What Do Ya Mean You're Still Single?

Roxy Siren

Copyright © 2024 Roxy Siren
All rights reserved. ISBN: 979-8-89324-072-6
Printed in the United States of America.

No part of this publication shall be reproduced, transmitted, or sold in whole or in part in any form without the prior written consent of the author, except as provided by the United States of America copyright law. Any unauthorized usage of the text without express written permission of the publisher is a violation of the author's copyright and is illegal and punishable by law. All trademarks and registered trademarks appearing in this guide are the property of their respective owners.

For permission requests, write to the publisher, addressed "Attention: Permissions Coordinator," at the address below.

Amazon Book Publishing Center 420 Terry Ave N, Seattle, Washington, 98109, U.S.A

The opinions expressed by the Author are not necessarily those held by Amazon Book Publishing Center.

Ordering Information: Quantity sales and special discounts are available on quantity purchases by corporations, associations, and others. For details, contact the publisher at info@amazonbookpublishingcenter.com.

The information contained within this book is strictly for informational purposes. The material may include information, products, or services by third parties. As such, the Author and Publisher do not assume responsibility or liability for any third-party material or opinions. The publisher is not responsible for websites (or their content) that are not owned by the publisher. Readers are advised to do their own due diligence when it comes to making decisions.

Amazon Book Publishing Center works with authors, and aspiring authors, who have a story to tell and a brand to build. Do you have a book idea you would like us to consider publishing? Please visit AmazonBookPublishingCenter.com for more information

Welcome friends. I am cordially inviting you to be entertained by my thrilling dating past, which will more than likely have you feeling thankful if you have already found your special someone... At the very least, these calamities are sure to induce a chuckle, no matter age, race, gender, or religion.

I will preface this by stating that most of these experiences were of the "online dating" kind. All horrifying details and "you've gotta be kidding me" scenarios are not a reflection of any specific dating avenue, but suffice it to say, what you see is not always what you get – anyone in this online dating struggle can, without question, agree.

For me, a way to bring laughter and light to these disastrous encounters was to crown a nickname to the deserved subjects. In some instances, names had to be adjusted to promote anonymity. Some are more exciting than others, but they made the cut for a reason. You will notice moving forward that, in some cases, a "background" is imperative for a clear picture of the story being told. Roll with it. It's worth it.

DISCLOSURE: If you're an overly sensitive person who is unable to benignly giggle at the inadequacies of others, then you have 2 options here...close the book or lighten up and continue reading. I would suggest the latter.

Dedication

Dedicated to the woman who made me. Who taught me strength, self-worth, and intrinsic love beyond what we know and feel...Who always thought I would be a great wife and Mother...which is why I never gave up hope for my happily ever after.

"SHAKY NECK"

Source of the Merger: Blind date, eagerly arranged by my "hopeless romantic" coworker, Barb.

One of my favorites, hands down...but merely for the story, not the date itself.

My coworker Barb, a middle-aged woman with seemingly kind intentions, begs to set me up with someone she and her friend *met at a bar*. "He is just so adorable...he is your age, has his own place, his own business, he's tall with dark wavy hair, a nice build, and beautiful green eyes! He just really seems like he has it all together, no kids, no crazy exes, no baggage." So many thoughts in my brain in this instant...wow, is he all these things? What in the world is wrong with him? Could she be exaggerating? My body cringes – even my closest friends would understand, *they* would have difficulty making me feel *comfortable* with the idea of a setup. It is just not me. Sure, I'm picky (thankfully), but that's not it – I feel more anxiety with just the *thought* of this not working out because there's that 3rd party, mutual friend pressure, some type of invisible guilt being spread on thick before you even exchange numbers.

It's the Friday before Labor Day Weekend, 10+ years ago, when Barb lays this news on me. Deeeeep sigh...ughhh...ok. "Can I give him your number, please? He's so excited to meet you!" I'll never forget. I said yes and walked into my office solemnly. Within 10 minutes, the vibration of my cell, a foreign number...and here we go. Vigorous texts, one after another – I should have known. But I partake...my Mom's voice in my head, "Give everyone a chance, don't be quick to judge, keep an open mind." He painfully asks if I can be free that same night...*ummmm...* "no," I say. "How about Saturday or Sunday? Want to meet on Monday?" I responded by saying I work the weekend, so let's plan for Monday. Without warning and unsolicited, he sends a picture of himself, but not a selfie. I received a picture that someone took of him standing under a tree...in complete shade...as the sun was setting...with a hat on...*are ya picking up what I'm putting down?* I immediately feel the disappointment and dread the idea of Monday.

Monday...alright. I call my Mom early in the day to describe the photo he sent, "Ohhh boy, well maybe you shouldn't go. Do you think he's hiding something?" Like his face? Body? Height? Yes. Yes. And yes. "Just go to a place where you can excuse yourself to use the bathroom and sneak out the back!" Mom! No, that is not ever going to happen, I can't do that to another human...but I can't say I didn't think hard about the idea. The repercussions and bad karma, nah.

We agreed on 7pm, at a local spot – but I planned the "local" spot because it tends to be poorly lit, filled mostly with older men, local bar...where I would not know a soul, and more importantly, no one would pay attention to this awkward first date. But he did some research that morning and realized my "pick" was not going to be open for the holiday – the only place open was a very popular bar/restaurant in the same town that I live and work in. (Cringe) *Please sweet Jesus do not let anyone see me,* is all I kept thinking. "I'll come pick you up," he says. Politely, I declined and assured him I would meet him at 7pm. "How will I give you a kiss goodnight if you don't let me walk you to your door?" Nervously, I reply, "Ahh, don't worry about that, I never kiss on first dates anyway" – phew! A lie via text feels safer than one in person!

At 6pm, he texted to inform me of how crowded it was, "Are you there already?" (What the??) "No, I was just driving by." Lie. Now it's 6:50pm, and my heart is definitely racing as I pull into the crowded parking lot, but not for the right reasons...I just know this will be horrible, and I have zero ability to *fake* having a good time. I have never been successful at hiding what I feel, it's known by my face and body language, both a blessing and a curse. So, this shall be fun. As soon as I put my car in park, my phone rings.... "Is that you in the black car?" – "Uhhh...hi, yes, I have a black car." – "OK, stay right there. I'll drive over." Headlights fly on, and a massive diesel truck charges through a parking lot of people and pulls up next to me...tinted, lifted, the overcompensation was nauseating. I know, I know, that sounds harsh – and there are MANY men out there with massive diesel trucks that are tinted, lifted, flexed out, and exhausts everywhere that are *not* overcompensating... so relax! But I knew. I said to myself, "I bet this guy is gonna hop out of this truck like a little oompa loompa. What a waste of a cute outfit!"

He did just that. Anxiously *hopped* down into the parking lot, roughly 5'4", in a t-shirt, dirty shorts and flip-flops. The disappointment felt like a weighted blanket on my shoulders...the awkward but expected hug ensued, and we were off to the front doors of doom! We sat down at the closest table to the door, my pick, and I couldn't help but do a "once-over" – every SINGLE physical feature that Barb had described to me was non-existent. "Tall," nope. "Dark wavy hair," nope – he had male pattern baldness with a very short crew cut style. "Nice build," nope – I'm pretty sure my shoulders were broader than his. Short little chubby arms and fingers, and toes! "Green eyes," yes actually, they were green – but nothing about them was attractive to me. Yes, I sound horrible... insulting... discriminating even. It's not necessarily that I don't like shorter men or bald men – because I do – but I don't enjoy the lie, and in this case, Barb's inaccuracy. But this is why *I pick what I like, nobody else can pick for me.*

We move forward, somehow, in conversation. Within 20 minutes, I realized that *everything* Barb had said was false. How many drinks had she had *before* this special being crossed her path? Again, unrequested, he told me that he is roughly 100K in debt because of "his crazy ex," who stole his boat. Without full details, he mentioned how he and his friend had "some trouble" with the police, so work is limited right now. If he was able to frequent a gym, well...I don't know that he would know what to do when in said gym. Oh, and he also hunts...bunnies and ducks...and pretty much stuffs *everything* he kills and hangs these trophies on the walls of his apartment. Charming. I also got an invitation to a duck dinner. Save me a seat.

I hope you feel what I am trying to convey, imagine sitting in that chair across from him, praying no one knows me, organizing my thoughts and words that I'll be spewing at Barb – and as I sit there, sipping my iced pint of beer and wishing I was anywhere else, I'm fixated on his *neck*. The entire time he spoke, and even any time he moved, his *neck* would *shake* quite elaborately. Once I saw it, I could see nothing else – it moved even when he took a breath. Now, the words of my Dad echoed in my head, "Whenever someone has an abnormality of some kind, just stare at their nose when you talk to them. Don't look anywhere else because they will know, and it can hurt their feelings." Dad, you were right, but man, it was mesmerizing! Horrifying, but couldn't get it out of my sight.

Now listen, the rest of this will be quick and painless – but you needed all the info to understand the nickname. He had never had the beer I was drinking, so he asked to sip mine. He liked it and continued to drink more of it. When the check came, I offered to split the bill, and he accepted the offer. In my silly mind, I thought this would make him realize that this would be our first and last outing. I always offer when the check comes because times are very different, and I do not want men to think I *expect* to be treated. But if I offer to go *Dutch* with you, this shall be our final goodbye. We walked to our vehicles, said good night (no kisses!), and left. Before I was even out of the parking lot, my phone was vibrating like crazy... "Our chemistry was so amazing, I felt like I could talk to you all night. This was the best first date I've ever had. I can't wait to see you again. Are you busy this weekend? Maybe we can make plans."

Were we on the same date? I mean, what? These types of texts are *awesome* when the feeling is mutual when clearly, you are both very attracted to each other, and the conversation is effortless. Those types of first dates flow so nicely, and you anxiously await the second date. Instead, I found myself drowning in a puddle of guilt and goo while still in the parking lot. *Ugh, is he watching me drive away? Will he follow?* I knew I had wasted a cute outfit!

Much to my embarrassment, I "ghosted" Shaky Neck without regard for his feelings. It was my first *ghosting,* and it haunted me, literally. For three weeks after our date, he texted, called, left voicemails, and texted pictures of activities he was planning with invitations to join. It was daily, feeling more like harassment, honestly…I couldn't take it. I chewed out Barb, who felt so awful afterward – but the damage had been done. I was unaware of how to block a number, but I wish I had. The final straw was when he sent me a picture of a 6-pack of the beer I was drinking that night – and wrote, "Grow up and call me." – this message was after multiple voicemails from him assuring me that I could *take my emotional walls down and enjoy myself, stop being so guarded*. So, I finally took down a wall, and called Shaky Neck, MD – and *opened up,* if you will. I'm sure he regrets challenging my emotions that day.

Years later, while out with friends – Shaky Neck and his entourage walk in. I lean over to my friends, "Oh no, Shaky Neck just walked in, gals." They all screamed aloud at the same time with pure excitement and thrill, "No way, Shaky Neck?!" They had never laid eyes on him, and he lived up to my detailed description. It will *never* get old. Ever. Especially when he made his way over to me at the bar and said, "Hey, do I know you?" – Why yes, you tried to know me, Shaky…

"GLEN-TENSE"

SOURCE OF THE MERGER: ONLINE

Glen's profile online was slightly deceiving, shocking, I know. But this was quite early in my online dating exposures before I was able to read between the lines. We messaged only a few times prior to exchanging numbers – an amateur move. I've realized over the years that I can detect a serious personality conflict in only a few messages back and forth on a dating app... do I sound crazy and judgmental? Yes. Have I been right? Yes. Have I continued to exchange numbers with said individuals? Yes. So, I get what I get, and I don't get upset.

He seemed quite anxious to meet, presumably to discern if I was *real*, and if my profile stood to be true. Ironically, *his* was not. Yes, he was an engineer according to his college degree, but he had not been employed for some time. Yes, he was divorced, according to the profile, but not emancipated – as he had been living with his parents, for some time also. These were not outstanding red flags in the "get to know me" game, but they were facts all the same for this 45-year-old, which he delivered slowly via text prior to the meeting. These facts posed an uneasy feeling and halted further questioning initially, so I decided to *just go with it*.

Our first date was in the summer, at an outside restaurant, roughly 1000°F, direct sun, but surprisingly not much disappointment. I could tell he was nervous as he kindly interrogated me, confirming all the checkboxes from the app as well as the narrative. "Wow, you seem just like your profile says." ...Why yes, yes, because I wrote my profile with the full intention of being truthful because otherwise, I would have to squirm during these questions and evade the truth. **Online Dating Tip #1:** When completing your profile, *be truthful*. If you're embarrassed by your true response, then leave it blank...then we all can scratch our heads and wonder what the real answer is...but do not lie. Especially about height! It is obviously a dead giveaway the moment you meet. Even if you are amazing, the lie is what we cannot relinquish.

Glen and I had 3 more dates within the following 2 weeks, which was more than I typically would be available for simply because of my schedule. He wanted to see me more often than that, but I worked every day, played sports, and had my own little life, too... you know the deal. Glen had nothing other than working out and the thought of plans with me. He spoke constantly about what our life would be like if we were to marry. He even asked me if I would take his name or hyphenate mine. Too soon. Wayyyy too soon. I shut down these thoughts delicately, but wow, he was intense. Even our kisses were crazy intense like he was inhaling my soul.... It was very one-sided, though, I didn't feel passion toward him. And for all those who feel women enjoy early conversations about marriage and children, I can confidently refute that thought. Sure, we enjoy the *thought* that someone might potentially *pick* us for life, who wouldn't?? – but make no mistake, unless you have a good chance of being "the one" in our eyes, it can be a game changer and may lead to a loss of attractiveness.

A close friend was throwing her annual summer party, so I thought to myself – maybe I should bring him and see how he interacts, as I was still trying to get to know him. A fun, outside party, people everywhere, children, distraction... where I can sit back and observe, and my friends can judge simultaneously. Eh, what the heck.

Crash. And. Burn.

Because the party was close to his residence (Mom & Dad's), I offered to pick him up. As soon as we entered the house, every move he made and the words he spoke should have led me out the door. Within 7 minutes, Glen had brazenly entered their kitchen, opened the fridge, proceeded to take out a beer, opened it, and chugged the bottle like he hadn't consumed a beverage for days. I stood, cemented to the floor...horrified. What kinda...who in the...how can I... My Mom's voice again, "Maybe he was nervous, it could have been just to calm him, he's meeting your friends for the first time. Maybe that's too stressful?" Oh, Ma, you are too nice.

Within 3 hours, I had had enough – multiple back-handed compliments to the host/hostess, inquisitions about the food on my plate, "Is that your second plate? It's a good thing you ran today", as I had my second portion of salad! As most people know, it is quite disrespectful to draw attention and judgment to a woman's plate (fellas and ladies), especially when you yourself had just indulged in a Big Mac snack at 2am that morning. Suffice it to say, this was our last outing. Clearly, the alcohol had caught up to him as I drove him home, he was completely unaware of verbal and social cues on this drive. Upon arrival at his Mom & Dad's, Glen would not exit my vehicle. Gently, I said, "I'm sorry, Glen, this will be the last time we see each other," blah blah blah. He cried. I am not exaggerating. He wailed for a solid 10 minutes while lying on my shoulder, "I can't even picture my life without you!" – Briskly, after peering at my watch, I stated, "Well, go back about 4 weeks ago when you didn't even know me, you were doing just fine! Now, please get out!"

There were no harassing texts or calls and no known drive-by incidents that I was aware of. But his intensity was enough to award him his name, Glen-tense. Six months later, he showed up in the lobby of the building where I work, asking the front desk to place a call to me, "Just tell her it's a friend who's visiting." As I approached the lobby, a trembling, diaphoretic Glen-tense, appearing to have aged 5 years, was walking toward me...both hands in the air, repeatedly saying, "Don't freak out, don't freak out, please don't freak out." The outlandish fib of him *being in the neighborhood* was entertained for what felt like forever, but after 4 minutes, I excused myself. My knees shook the entire way back to my office, just a little reminder that *crazy* could be around the corner, always be ready...however, I was in stilettos, which can always double as a weapon if warranted. He proceeded to head to the parking lot and sent an email to our Relations department praising me for being gracious enough to put my day on hold to make sure his needs were met. Because the manager and I were friendly, she called me immediately about the email – and in 2 minutes, I was in her office rattling off the story of Glen-tense...she was more petrified than I was with his shameless visit, insisting Security be aware of this incident. I cannot make this up.

"GRAVE JOHN"

Source of the Merger:
Close Family Member's Friend

I was introduced to John when I was 22 before online dating was even *a thing*. I had spent 4 days in Florida with a family member, her boyfriend, and John. Apparently, he was interested, but he waited until we landed back home to ask for my number. He was *allllright*, a personality like a dry mop though, stoically serious – and even on vacation, it seemed difficult for him to let loose and have fun – not my style. **Dating Tip #2:** Leave your guilt at the door in regards to agreeing to dates just because there's a family member connection. Even if they set up a date – no matter how close your relationship may be, if you are not genuinely interested in the person, then say no!

I was away at college when John and I connected, he had to travel far for our first date, so it took a hot minute to set up. He worked for the government and had a crazy schedule, but he was seemingly able to text and call me constantly, almost every waking minute for the 2 weeks prior to our date. Don't get me wrong, if feelings are mutual, the frequency of communication is never an issue...this had a clinger vibe, and boy, do I hate it when I'm right! To give credit where it's due, he definitely took the reins to set up a great first date – a fantastic restaurant on the water, setting the scene for sure. It was summer, so I had worn a sundress, while John had made the 2-hour drive in a suit, a bit more dapper than myself. A challenging part of his personality, though, was his level of seriousness - he was so serious all the time, not only in his attire but in all aspects of his life. This made it difficult for me to be *me*, I was constantly masking my personality – barely anything made him smile, and next to nothing made him laugh...what a great way to start a relationship. He would occasionally speak about family and only had a few friends – he mostly mentioned just his Mom, but even then, there was zero warmth in his voice. I couldn't tell if he was trying to portray a *tough guy* or if he was just always serious. And each time we hung up the phone, I felt zapped of positivity. A tiny red flag was noted.

We arrive at the restaurant, and John turns to me and says, "I need you to carry my gun for me." *Excuse me, what?* My words were somewhat garbled, but I was asking for clarification. *What in the world? Why does he need a gun on him during dinner? Is this legal? Will it fit in my purse?* He went on to say the gun must be on his person at all times, which I've come to learn is *not* true, but then again, this was 20 years ago easily.

So what did I do?? I buttoned my naïve lips, fumbled the first gun I'd ever held into my purse, and pulled the zipper closed, silently praying it would remain closed until we came back to the car. Thankfully, it was not needed during dinner. The tiny red flag was now multiplying.

We had a few glasses of wine, which opened him up a bit – but when we came back to my apartment, he seemed a bit too loose. The plan was for him to stay the night, so I wasn't shocked when he started to change his clothes. But halfway through, he began to fall asleep, almost mid-sentence. So, I just pulled the covers over him and slid in next to him to fall asleep. He put his arms around me and said, "I'm totally in love with you." He kissed me on the cheek and closed his eyes. *Oh boy.* This is a different type of red flag...*in love?* Come onnn...was it the nice steak dinner? The wine? Dessert? – I mean, it could not have been my charismatic personality because it's been tucked away since we met. The next morning, I had silently hoped that either his words were exaggerated due to intoxication or he would have forgotten he had spoken them due to intoxication... either way, I would have felt much less guilty about dismissing his feelings. I kept it light and breezy, and it was never addressed when he left.

We continued to text and speak, but the personality differences were extreme, in addition, I could feel my clinger vibe accelerating. I agreed to one... final... date, although he wasn't aware this would be final. Here's the plan, or so I thought...Come back home to my parent's house from college for a night, guaranteeing *no sleepover*. Hit a restaurant, go see my sister at her work, limit alone time, then go back home – bingo-bongo-done! John pulls up to my parents' house wearing white boat shoes with a matching white leather belt – does the rest of the outfit even *matter* at this point? Unfortunately, the obligatory handshake with Dad was unavoidable, but it was short and sweet, and off we went! Dinner was benign, and ironically, there was no need to harness a gun for this meal, which was a positive. I was happy to be going to visit my sister since she knew him and could be a good buffer for me. When we started driving, he told me we needed to stop back at his Mom's house, where he also lived, unbeknownst to me. Hey guys, if you still live at home, mention it! But my first thought was, *oh no, I have to meet his Mom now? Ugh, this is awful.* Now relax, relax – I *love* Moms, and typically, Moms like me back – but this situation just felt icky in my belly.

It was dark by this time. We pull up in the driveway, where I had hoped I could stay while he "picked up something."

John: "Come in with me."

Me: "Really?"

John: "Yes, really. You don't want to?"

Me: "No, it's not that, I just feel like it's late, and I feel awkward meeting your Mom this late."

John: "Well, it doesn't matter how you feel, I want you to come in with me."

Me: "……" A long, awkward stare ensued.

Truly, I had no idea how to react, but I know I just kept thinking *tough it out this will be the last time you see him*. We don't enter the front door, he channels me around the back, in the dark, to slip into a deck/patio door. As loud as the sliding glass doors were, there wasn't a sound inside or a light for that matter. I stood eerily on a door mat where I felt my shoes were glued. All I could see in the distance was a dim oven light in the kitchen, but neither of us was moving toward it. Then, "Mother!" John's stern, loud, command-ish voice called through the house, which made my spine straighten immediately – setting an uncomfortable tone to the dark room. I wait. I hear nothing in response. John appears annoyed but still hasn't moved a foot. "Mother, where are you?!" – Even louder, authoritatively, abrasively. I can then hear her feet shuffling, and her silhouette appears in front of the oven light. I cannot see a face, but her posture and presence appear frightened but obedient. Remember those red flags??

John: "Mother, I need you to get me the box from the safe."

Mom: "The box?"

John: (Annoyed) "Yes, Mother. You put the box I had in the safe for me. I need it now!"

Mom: "OK, John, I'll get it."

What in the world is in this BOX? I mean, I can pretty much guarantee it's not a gun because John casually walks around with those. Now my feet were truly glued to the floor, body completely erect with fear – firstly, how in the holy hell does someone speak to their Mother this way, and their name is not Norman Bates from Psycho? And in front of a stranger? I wasn't even introduced (thank goodness). Secondly, what could be in this box that we *needed* to drive back to the house for?

As soon as it was handed over, I walked my shaking knees back to the vehicle and stepped in. He followed with a deep, annoyed sigh. "So, what happened there?" I asked. It was the first time I even questioned his stoic side, but I just felt I had to. He handed me the box and told me to open it. It's a jewelry box – and yes, lots of gals would be excited for a sweet gift on the second date. But try to understand my mindset because you're currently thinking I'm ungrateful... let's review: dry mop personality, clinger, has me carry a firearm on date #1, loves me after date #1, berates his Mom in front of me on date #2, still without introducing me...and now, a gift. I slowly opened the box to find a gold necklace with a large gold heart embracing a purple stone and matching earrings. *Was it something I would wear?* No, absolutely not. I rarely wore gold, and this item had a very childish design. *Did I thank him over and over for it?* Yes. *Was that enough?* No. I closed the box and leaned in to kiss him, but he immediately questioned why I wasn't putting the jewelry on. My response was a thorough explanation, leaving out the truth, which I thought would suffice. *I'm sorry, John, it's just that I'm wearing silver tonight, and I have a one-shoulder dress on, so I typically don't wear a necklace when I wear a one-shoulder.... blah blah blah.*

Instant anger. Instant disappointment. Oh, and he would not take no for an answer. He grabbed the box, took the necklace out, put it around my neck and said, "Well, you're going to wear it tonight." The next couple of hours were a complete blur. When I saw my sister, she instantly knew something was not right after I shot her the *crazy eyes*. But it was impossible to slip her a mention of the story because he never left my side, not even to use the bathroom! I was so shocked at his behavior that even to this day, I can't recall how we stopped talking or if I was honest with him after that night. I just know I counted down the minutes until he brought me back to my parent's house, which is opposite to what I should have felt. Almost twenty years later he sees my profile on an online site and sends a message – "Hey, how have you been?"

– Imagine the gall...the strange memories of John were instant discomfort, like being pushed into a freezing cold pool. No thanks, Grave John, I choose life.

Whatever happened to the necklace and earrings, you're wondering? I sold it back to a jewelry store when gold was at its highest price. Satiating.

"MASSIVE MIKE"

Source of the Merger: Online

A fan favorite.

I met Michael over 15 years ago. He was the second guy I had met online, so yes, I was unseasoned, naïve and way too trusting. His profile online professed a very wholesome man – a kind smile, active in the Army, and even had a yellow Labrador in his pictures. We spoke every night for a couple weeks before we met in person – great personality and good conversation. He checked quite a few of "the boxes," but now for the reveal. He lived out of state, so his commute was over an hour.

Considerately, or so I thought, I offered that he come to my house, and then I would drive to dinner. As a positive, he was thoughtful in his plan...he knew I liked Pinot Noir, so when he chose the restaurant, he looked at their wine menu and purchased a bottle of the same wine offered at the restaurant on his ride. Hey guys, that takes consideration, time, and planning...so take notes!

I peered through the blinds, anxiously awaiting his arrival. A vehicle pulled up with his state tags, and immediately, I had butterflies! However, when he stepped out of the truck, those butterflies fell flat. I was mistaken, or was I? The extremely large man, much larger than his pictures portrayed, began walking toward my door carrying wine and wilted flowers. Who was this? Michael had blonde hair, not brown...He had a nice build wrapped in fatigues on his profile; that's not who I see right now. Not again... another cute outfit wasted!

The doorbell rings, even though I have been frozen on the other side of the door for a few moments. I barely opened the door to fake my best smile when he barreled through, stating, "Ugh, do you know how much traffic I just sat in? You're totally driving to dinner!" The buttons on his powder blue button-down were busting at the seams; it was so hard not to notice. He was solidly 80-100lbs heavier than his pictures, had longer brown hair, and was older than his photos from the profile. I kindly leaned in for a *friend-hug*, as I was unable to fake any other emotion. Frantically, I thanked him for the flowers, grabbed them, and led him to the kitchen to place them in water. He kept talking. I cannot even recall what he was saying, but I noticed he was tucking the bottom of his jeans *into* his Dr. Martens shoes...*into* the shoes!

Me: "What are you doing to your jeans?"

Mike: "I'm just trying to tuck them in, they're so long."

Me: "I see that, but why inside the shoes? Why not cuff them or something?"

Mike: "Yeah, but it's better this way, they'll stay in there all night."

Me: "Looks like they're a solid 6 inches too long, how about a shorter inseam?"

I know, God forgive me, but how do these things happen? Where is the rationale? And as a person incapable of hiding an emotion on my face, how can I fake this all night? I try to hustle us out of the house, *the quicker we get there, the quicker I'll never see him again*. Roughly 30 seconds on the road, and Mike says, "Hey, can we stop at Bed, Bath and Beyond on the way to dinner? I need a new shower curtain." Whatttttt. Surely, maybe we'll pick up a scale, too, because when you offered me the information of you being 6'2" and 200lbs, I believed that. **Online Dating Tip #3:** Refer to Tip #1 – the lies are horrid! But also, do not offer information when it's not requested – I would never ask someone what they weigh…I'm a woman, we despise that question. We enter BB&B, pass the scales and grab a curtain. The subtle comment from Mike, "Look, we're already looking at home décor together,"…sweet Jesus, no, we're not Mike. Off to dinner, we go! While en route, hand to God, Mike says, "Hey, you know what's funny? I jumped on the scale this morning, and I feel so bad…remember when I told you I was 200lbs?" *Keep your eyes on the road, nod politely, I tell myself…* "It turns out I'm 216lbs, I don't know when that happened!" The tiniest, forced smile came across my face, but still never took my eyes off the road… "Wow…yea, that's funny, haha." Nope. *Is that a joke?* I mean, I don't travel with a carnival guessing weights, but I can call bullshit when I hear it. In fact, I would guess he was an easy 300lbs. He was better off saying nothing…not one word.

We got to the restaurant, but our table wasn't ready yet, so we ordered a glass of wine and sat in the crowded waiting area…I hoped no one would recognize me, as usual. I snatched the bill for the wine when the hostess brought it over, but a thank you wasn't heard – instead, Mike said, "Well, I would hope you would pay for this, I mean, I'm going to be buying the dinner!" Deeeeep sigh…deep sigh…bite your tongue…little smile, this should be over soon.

We finally sat for dinner in the center of the dining room, close to a live tree and plant display, I recall wishing I could dive into this decor. Luck would have it that our waitress was my intern at the time and was very excited to witness me on a date. Obviously,

I had to introduce him against my will. He proceeded to order pretty much everything on the menu, including unlimited refills on wine. I am fortunate I was driving and was unable to continue drinking because if not, I would have guzzled wine and called an Uber…which would have been disrespectful, as it would have been a solo ride. After he enjoyed the taste of 3 desserts, he continued to enjoy the wine. His voice was boisterous, drawing attention to us, which I disliked whether the date was good or bad. He pushed himself backwards, rocking on the back two legs of his chair, dipping his head into the tree behind him, where he proceeded to smack the leaves around and make noises. Gently, I said, "Mike, you look like a gorilla in the jungle. Can you please stop?" Dear. Lord.

The ride home was unmemorable, but as soon as we entered my foyer, he turned and said, "Hey, do you have another shirt I can change into? I think I ate too much". Clearly, this ensemble was "fitted" from the start. Blankly, I look at him and say, "I don't think I have anything that would fit, but I can look." Other than my oversized robe, I had a large green t-shirt that I used to paint, which I gave him. Ironically, it fits like paint. I could see every outline of his abdomen and waistline, but he was more comfortable – after all, cotton is forgiving. He proceeded into the kitchen and asked to open the wine he had brought over. Now, as a compliment, Michael did plan a bit. By purchasing the same Pinot Noir from the restaurant, his plan was to continue the evening at my home. I entertained the opening of the bottle; God knows I needed it! But after a glass, I mentioned that he should be "getting on the road" since his drive is a bit long. Mike says, "Oh, I thought I could stay here with you overnight." Oh. Boy. **Online Dating Tip #4:** Do not ever, ever, ever let them "pick you up" or meet at your house until their sanity is firmly established. Even if they are chivalrous, precautions are necessary for this exact reason. Sorry, Mike, no vacancies tonight.

I could not entertain conversation after this date – and it was difficult to fake a "liking," so I just cut it off. Weeks later, he contacted me online again and was beside himself, "I don't know where we went wrong. I thought we had a great time." The right thing for me at that time was to ignore the messages because I was taught *if you don't have anything nice to say, don't say anything*. I guess a bad day got the better of me, which led me to reply to yet another message from Mike. I outlined the lies…the *dated* picture online of his dog stood out, as he told me on our date (after some wine) that his Labrador had passed away 5 years prior. I mentioned other fibs, including the deception of his age (he was 4 years older than stated), his weight, and even his hair was a completely different color. Surprisingly, though, Mike didn't take it well, in fact, he attempted to defend his deception, which was even more unattractive. So, I made it easy, Block, Delete. I learned.

"BORING BRAD"

SOURCE OF THE MERGER: ONLINE

Brad's profile was desirable to merely peruse. The type of physical presence that drew me in...*tall...handsome...nice eyes...nice smile*...and the *shoulders!* He absolutely checked those attraction boxes – but after being let down in the past, I wasn't expecting these pictures to match the being.

We exchanged numbers early and began to plan a first date. We had never spoken, but I did enjoy the banter between us via text – which is another telltale of personalities meshing...*or not*. As usual, I leave it up to the man to decide on the first date. I'm pretty easygoing when it comes to being open to an activity versus sitting down at a bar and staring at one another when first meeting. There's usually so much undesired pressure on the first date, so why not break the ice and *do* something instead of sitting stagnant, eyeing each other up? Brad chooses bowling. Oh boy. I do love activities...friendly competition...interaction – don't get me wrong. But bowling presents an entirely different path of anxiety, at least for me. Regardless of your gender, *what is the first thing you think of in this situation?* Well, I'll blurt it out in case you're struggling...*what am I going to wear to cover my butt??* As an aside, let us look at bowling's awkward circumstances. Roughly fifty percent of the time, your back (and your *full* back) is facing your date. This can only mean that half of the time you're spending together includes them looking at your heinie. Yes, is anyone also affirming this thought? In addition, when you competitively release your bowling ball, the position you are forced into...a twisted lunge, if you will...jets out said heinie, even further. Then, once releasing your ball, you must gracefully pull your lunged legs back to the starting position. *Gracefully*. And yes, some of you are rolling your eyes, completely enamored by my overly critical thoughts – but I'm quite sure you'll never bowl the same again without thinking of this story... especially if it's on a date! Let's not forget to mention that whether one pin or ten pins are leveled, the proverbial, sweaty-handed "high five" ensues. But yes, yes, let us do this on our first date. I am in. We met at a popular bowling alley in the city, but its main attraction, oddly enough, is not bowling. Here, there are only about 8 lanes to bowl, a large bar, and at least 10 pool tables. Brad's presence is all that his profile depicted; all the eye-pleasing positives were confirmed. He seemed very quiet compared to his texting personality, but no doubt this may be nerves, so I thought. The wait was over an hour – so we grabbed a drink at the bar and headed over to the pool tables to kill some time.

Another splendid, rear-focused activity to kick the night off! There are *zero* safe positions in pool. I took a long sip of my beer, threw care to the wind, and grabbed a stick.

An hour later, I had beaten Brad 4 times in pool. Four times. The *quietness* I had mistaken for nerves turned into a stern brow with scant conversation. *Was he mad?* I'm not even good! But he clearly was worse. After each game, I tried to keep it light and say flirty things, but Brad would have none of it. Hey guys – you don't have to *ever* let us win, but don't be mad if we win on our own accord, either. It's pool...nobody is paying attention...it's not like the score is posted above the table, in red lights, with our names. So dramatic. But alas, we are saved by the bell! They call us because our lane is open, and we're ready to bowl. A soft smile crossed Brad's face. Man, he was handsome when he smiled. Boring, but handsome.

Another hour and a half of brutal defeat, as unfortunately, I won our 3 rounds of bowling. *This was awful*. I cannot recall even *thinking* about how my *heinie* looked or if my lunge was graceful or not. All I can remember is stressfully stepping up to the approach area and praying not to throw a strike. I mean, sure, I could purposely throw it into the gutter...but that's not in my DNA. There were no "high-fives," no smiles, no banter. Brad was stone-faced and appeared disappointed. Not disappointed in his own lack of talent, though, the eyes he gave me were of complete disdain. Again, I struggled trying to lighten the mood and carry on conversation...basic interaction and *getting to know someone* was impossible during this game. There *was* no personality, looking at his face mimicked watching paint dry. But let's be honest, Brad, if I beat you, scoring 90, maybe you should practice, no? If you don't want to practice, then work on catching a personality. Different than our pool table disaster, bowling scores were *indeed* above our lane, in red lights, with our names next to them. The loud screech of Velcro helped to communicate his disgust as he ripped his dilapidated bowling shoes off.

A year later, Brad reached out to meet again. Yes, his number was still in my phone, and will forever remain in my phone for this very reason. When these clowns feel horny and bored, your phone will vibrate, and it would be beneficial for you to *know* the number. He ended up explaining to me that he was "annihilated" on our first date. Attempting to explain that his poor behavior and lack of interaction were because he had been drinking with his buddies the entire day before we met up at night. Ironically, though, Brad did not blame his suboptimal performance on alcohol, maybe that was the most real part. Do not do this, guys or gals. If you're nervous, and a shot or sip may take the edge off, indulge. But if getting hammered is your chosen avenue before embarking on a first date, then you might have an issue. Thanks for the compliment, Brad.

"JOE TOES"

Source of the Merger:
Set-up from a Friend

Joe was a referral from a close friend of mine, related to her through marriage. He was 28 when we met – an established, chivalrous and handsome man...great personality, was very sweet, owned his own home, and was self-employed – he was a complete package! Joe lived about an hour away, so for our first few dates, we met at halfway points for dinner. After a month or so, we had planned for him to come to my home for the first sleepover. He had a thriving, family-owned business, which kept him very busy – but in the winter, they closed, so he would sell Christmas trees before the holiday. The first "sleepover" date happened to be on my birthday, and he was going to drive down after work. Naively, I pictured him arriving, showering, us going to dinner... some wine, going back home for a movie, etc. However, when I opened the door, I found Joe covered in sap, sweatpants, a hoodie, work boots...and *no* change of clothes, not even a toothbrush, did Joe pack.

I tried not to look disappointed, after all, this was a super new relationship, and I should not have expected *plans,* even though it is very attractive when a plan is made! *So,* I ordered dinner for us because, clearly, we were not heading out anywhere. After he showered, we were lying on the couch, and I couldn't help but notice that he had put his dirty socks back on his feet. What. Is. Going. On.

Me: "Joe, why don't you take those socks off? They're dirty, and you put them back on?"

Joe: "Yeah, I always keep my socks on, I don't like my feet."

Immediately, my brain begins to churn, like a browser with six tabs open...*what is inside of those socks?!* I don't personally enjoy feet, but I've never met a male who admitted they did not care for their own feet, so this was mysterious to me. Joe begins to chuckle as I get up, make a move for his feet, and slowly pull off one of the socks. I gasped and dropped the sock on the floor...

Me: "Joe! What is going on with your feet? Your toenails? What's happening here?"

Joe began to giggle, it sounded quite adorable, actually...he wasn't embarrassed at all with the appearance of his 28-year-old feet, which appeared to be an 85-year-old's neglected toes and toenails. His toenails were yellow, extremely long and crusted. "Joe, you could wear a smaller size shoe if you cut these nails!" All he could do was smile and laugh, he couldn't even respond through his laughter – and my mind was blown! The questions were endless for me, my brain could not organize quick enough...

Me: "What do you do in the shower? Why are they yellow? I think they may be infected. Are your nails sensitive? How come you haven't cut them? Does it hurt when you try? How come your toes are so dry? Are you soaking them? Are you washing between your toes?"

Then I took a breath and looked his way – we laughed hysterically for a solid 10 minutes. But then, he answered a few of my questions honestly. "I hate cutting my toenails, they're too thick to cut. No, I do not wash between my toes, the soapy water from my body runs down and washes my feet automatically." Whattttt?? Whyyy?? And Howww?? I went into straight *teach-back* mode...

Me: "So, you don't wash your toes?"

Joe: "No."

Me: "And you don't wash your feet?"

Joe: "No."

Me: "Do you use soap at all down there?"

Joe: "Yes, whatever washes down."

Me: "Do you realize you might have an infection?"

Joe: "No, but maybe."

Me: "Do you want to lose any toes at the age of 28?"

Joe: "No."

Me: "Does your Mom know you don't wash your toes?"

Joe: "Hahahhah, I don't think so, no."

He laughed the *entire* time through this awful interrogation – and God love him, he was a great sport. But I knew what I had to do. Despite this being the day of my birth, I hopped up off the couch, grabbed his hand and drug him unwillingly to the bathroom, sat his ass on the side of the tub, and scrubbed his feet. The laughing was uncontrollable and was the only consolation as I was close to crying, wondering about what *else* he may not be cleansing on his body! He was incredibly ticklish, so it was quite a task, but I scrubbed between his toes also! We both laughed, but I was advising at the same time… "It wouldn't tickle if you were the one cleaning your own toes!" It ended up being an overall enjoyable night, albeit an unromantic one. Joe Toes was his name, unequivocally.

He was such a good sport when it came to this name; our friends and my family were aware of the details, and he laughed whenever it was mentioned. We were dating on and off but had reunited at said friend's wedding, where Joe told me he washed his toes specially for that night, which left us both in tears laughing. He went on to tell me he needed a toenail removed because of fungus…Boy, I hate it when I'm right.

"BIBLE BRIAN"

Source of the Merger: Online

Brian's profile was relatively straightforward online. His pictures were all *accurate* and seemed to reflect his personality. He was undoubtedly tall, and his job was *real*, those were the simple things I found were most often lied about on online profiles. There were no hidden secrets that I knew of or would come to find out in the first month because that's how long this one lasted. Typically, crazy little secrets would begin to seep out within the first 4-6 weeks (give or take) while I got to know some of these dates. Some secrets were as simple as admitting they never protected their rears from public restroom toilets, like ever...they boasted about sitting raw on the toilet... but why? Other secrets included sharing a car with their sister *for a few years*, being closet drinkers, and being once-in-a-while showerers. You get it, and it is inevitable. Some of them are not "non-negotiables," but others clearly are. Yes, these are the things that seep out, as most of the dating world knows.

Back to Brian...Brian was very religious, overly so sometimes, meaning that he thanked God for everything...constantly. God's grace was mentioned in our daily conversations, text messages, to strangers we sat next to in a comedy club, he even thanked God while kissing. I mean, I believe in God – but it became a little much when I was awakened by the melodic voice of Joel Osteen on the TV and forbidden to change the channel. A positive thing about Brian, though, was that he thought *everything* I did was *heavenly*, like everything. The eggs I cooked were a gift from God – "Only an angel could wear that dress," he once said. "God brought us together, we even drive the same car. Should we just head to the chapel now?"... Ahhhh. It was a lot, a whole lot.

The day of Brian's demise was not foreseen. I knew there were traces of an overbearing quality, meaning I didn't have to guess if he liked me. But *too much, too quick* is not a quality that I am attracted to. No, no, no...you're thinking, *of course, all women like when men play hard to get*. Nope, I do not love that either. I would just thoroughly appreciate a man reading the room if you will. For instance, if you text me how much you might miss me after one week of dating, and I breezily respond with a smiley face, that means pumping the brakes. It isn't *code* for *trying harder,* and it doesn't warrant the response of, "Can I just drive over for a hug?" No. Indeed my hugs are damn good, but sadly Brian, you cannot.

My friend from work was having a Memorial Day BBQ, and I decided after 3 weeks that Brian would be a safe +1 to bring and introduce to a few of my colleagues. He mingled to the best of his ability but made a better shadow for me than a +1. My location was irrelevant to him...under a tree, on the bench, down at the dock, kitchen, porch, bathroom – Brian was in step at all times. Relatable to a tall, blue-eyed gnat. It was a beautiful sunny day. Everyone was having a great time – good music, good people, and good drinks. We were drinking an orange punch, super bright orange and phenomenally delicious, made by my friend Kevin, the pride of Jamaica. Maybe it was too delicious for Brian. We were talking, holding our punch, when he leaned in and said, "Hey, you have pretty orange specs in your eyes right now..." I giggled and countered, "I think that might just be the reflection of the punch." Brian does not hesitate, "Well, if having orange specs in your eyes means that you're falling in love, then I have them too." Wait. A. Minute.

Now, that's either an award-winning line that he was waiting to dose, or I have completely lost all sense of what is *normal* to say within a 3-week timeframe of dating. Within seconds, I knew this would be our last event together. It is not to dispute that some couples truly find love that quickly – but typically, the *love* they feel is mutual and reciprocated... I have experienced falling in love that quickly in the past, so I know it exists. I'm aware of the many people who may think I sound like a cynical, ungrateful woman who would never appreciate a good man. Although I did love that punch, not so much the inference of its meaning... The letdown was not taken so well by Brian, but my only offering was that maybe I wasn't the one God sent him to spend his life with. He was easily folded.

"FBI FRANK"

Source of the Merger: Online

The longest, and to-date, the greatest compilation of no-nos in less than a month's time

Frank was an early communicator, and I mean early! Within the first 2 hours of exchanging messages via the online dating site, Frank insisted upon a phone call "to make sure our personalities would mesh well," he claimed. **Online Dating Tip #5:** Eassssy Tiger with the phone number request on the second message and early phone call mandate. I, too, dislike the idea of a "pen pal" when first exchanging pleasantries online, and I am utterly aware that the back and forth can be exhausting, especially if you're not on the site daily. Correspondence is sometimes work, but I can assure you that if our personalities do not mesh, it's going to happen early – and most likely during the first few messages online. Not everyone wants to give their number out that quickly, only to regret it.

The phone call commences, as I'm running around doing chores in my house... I wasn't ready, I wasn't ready! But I had to answer, how could I have been communicating back and forth via cell but not answer the call? Great personality, is super easy to talk to and has high hopes for the meshing of personalities. Frank lives roughly an hour away, so coordinating schedules for meeting halfway began – but, to compliment Frank, he had offered to drive all the way to me...this never happens! So, I take him up on the offer – it's set for 8:30pm at a local diner, see you then! Now, typically, 8:30 is super late to begin a date in my eyes, plus I get up at 5:30am for work...but I'm rolling with it, also assuming this date will not include food, however, so I eat beforehand.

Frank did *not* disappoint! H-a-n-d-s-o-m-e, dark hair with a remarkable fade, dark eyes, a smoothly shaven chiseled jaw, neat as a pin, amazing smile, and smelled even better than he looked! We sat down at a booth and started to get acquainted as the waitress arrived. I kindly just ordered a hot tea, it felt too late for coffee. Frank proceeds to order soup, salad, and a full dinner. I struggled not to show shock, but my face just did not cooperate. Frank offers, "I usually eat dinner at this time anyway when I get home from the gym." Noted. I ended up ordering a cup of soup just to "fit in."

To skip ahead, our next 2 dates were similar...8:30pm, he ate meals each time. To be clear, the only reason the dates were this late was because he refused to skip the gym on the one night per week in which we made plans. I playfully requested, "Hey, since I get up early for work, do you think one night you could skip the gym so we could meet around 7?" His response was, "Not unless you want me to be grumpy, I need to go every day, or I'm miserable." Noted (again).

So, date #4 – ends up being a Saturday...I'm sure the time will be different! I offered to drive towards him since every previous date was in my area. Frank invites me to his home, "We can BBQ on my grill, just come here." "Sounds great, what time?" "How's 8:30?" – Really. Of course, I sent the proverbial passive-aggressive "lol" in return, but he was serious. I talked myself out of my immediate funk – *so we're going to start to BBQ at 8:30? What time will this said food hit my plate?* Geez, now I just sound like an old lady.

It's 7:15pm, and I'm on my way – I stop at the liquor store to pick up a 6-pack to bring because he tells me he has the food covered. "Just bring something to drink." Got it. I slowly turn down his street and look at the clock, realizing it's 8:20pm, so I'm just a bit early...but I don't see his car in the driveway. I mean, it's dark out, but I'm quite sure it was empty. As I passed the house, I noticed his car flying through the stop sign and coasting into the driveway. What. In. The. *Is he just getting home? Did he see me pass?* Oh No. I drove to the next street, turned, and waited in my car like a weirdo until it was 8:29pm, and then drove back around. As I walked up the driveway, I felt like I was at the wrong house. The lawn was burnt and uncared for...the blinds in each window were crooked, broken..., and the front screen door was hanging off the hinge... it was like a scene out of a horror movie. And a scene that I was invited to.

I brace myself, *what in the world am I walking into?* "Hello?" I say, looking in through the screen door – I see him running back and forth in the kitchen frantically...from the table to the sink, back to the table, then to the fridge. "Come on in!" he yells. *Come on in*, like we've been dating for months...4th date – I barely know your last name, Frank. Can you come to the door? He doesn't stop his hustle within the kitchen as I step in and awkwardly giggle. In fact, he screams, "Hey, just sit wherever you want, I'll be right there." As I stepped through the door, my entire body stiffened... completely erect and unbelievably sad simultaneously. *Oh no, ugh, whyyyyy*. **Dating Tip #6:** If you invite someone to your home, be ready for a human to be in your home – I would think this is common sense, but apparently not. I peered around the *(unlivable)* living room in complete and utter shock. Focusing first on the carpet, which may have been light gray at one point, was extremely soiled in high-traffic locations – leaving a *medium* gray tendency not to be out-darkened by the crumb-filled corners and dusty divots along the baseboards. The couches were white, and I use the term "were" and "white" quite honestly, as they were no longer – in fact, the couch closest to the door that I was going to risk my life planting my tush on was covered in a black sheet, not a mystery as to what could be underneath. The 1-seat sofa, which locked up the corner of the room, was mostly white, aside from the smut-coated arm and hand rests, which shined from the door. Behind this tragedy was an 8-bulb arc floor lamp that branched over the couch, but its purpose was to *dimly* light up the room, as only 2 of the bulbs were in working condition. In addition to the turmoil I was viewing, the black lacquer furniture was rampant, as it is for most Italians – I'm allowed to say this because I'm Italian, so don't take offense. Contrary to Italian culture, however, was the layer of dust across this furniture, which was at least a half-inch thick – covering the small decorations, the dried flowers placed about (yes, this was real), and the glass table tops. One thing I'm excellent at is being attentive, sometimes a blessing and sometimes a curse – and I paid *attention* to this entire room within the first 17 seconds under this roof. I did not know where to walk first, so I cautiously perused into the kitchen, where he was still moving swiftly. There was no greeting, no kiss on the cheek, no one-arm hug, nothing.

Me: "Hey! I brought some beer, should I put it in your fridge?"

Frank: "Oh, yeah, sure, I'm just making a protein shake – I just got back from the gym."

Totally acting as if I didn't know he just got home...

Me: "The gym? Is that why we're eating so late? Hahaha. You're making a shake? Oh no, you're not gonna be hungry for a while, and I'm starving!"

Frank: "No, no, I'll be fine...plus, the chicken is still frozen, so it has to thaw."

WHATTT. I mean, is this real? I should've bolted then, but I felt that would be rude... but isn't making a protein shake at 8:30pm in front of a hungry woman whom *you invited to come over so you could BBQ for*...RUDE? Yes, indeed, it is. Sternly, I walk toward the refrigerator because I would, at the very least, enjoy drinking a cold beer at some point, or 10! Another shocking discovery – there is literally *nothing else* in this refrigerator other than a pack of half-frozen chicken, a red pepper and an onion. There is *nothing else*. Not an egg? Water? Mustard? Old cheese? You're a 44-year-old man... you don't even have milk? How do you eat? As I walk, crumbs are crunching under my shoes – there must have been food here at some point, or was it the oats he just added to his protein shake?! Furious, just furious.

So now I'm trapped here. Hilariously, I was telling an ex of mine this story – he suggested at this point in the date that I should have made an excuse like, "I'll be right back, I just wanna grab a piece of gum from my car," and BOLTED! He was right, things got worse. After his shake is made, he asks me if I mind if he goes upstairs to shower, "Here, just pop a movie in, pick a DVD, and I'll put it on while I shower." I sat down on the sheeted (safest) couch in the room, "No, it's ok. I don't need to watch a movie, I'll just watch TV. It's fine." Come to find out, he didn't have cable – only channels 3, 6, and 10. *Where am I?* He ran up the stairs, oatmeal/protein shake in hand! And there I was, left in the house of horrors. I was petrified to even leave my purse on the carpet, so I held it on my lap. Fearful of some type of hidden "nanny" camera, I lock my head straight at channel 6... but move my eyes *everywhere I can*. As tragic as this room is with filth, it's also more fit for a teenager. The TV stand, if that's what we're calling it – had the entire cardboard back *cut* out of it with a jagged-edged knife in order to plug the cord into the electrical socket on the wall. *What am I seeing? Did he do this?* Keep your head straight, drop your eyebrows, and do NOT show emotion in case of the hidden camera. Don't ask me why I was fearful of a camera – I guess once I entered this house, I kept looking for a rolling camera and comedian to jump out and tell me, *"You've been punk'd."* Nope, this was real life.

It's now 8:50pm when he comes running down the stairs, freshly showered and *still* clinging to his half-consumed protein shake, wearing a Gold's Gym tank (insert eye roll). *When in the world are we eating?* He sits down next to me on the death couch, arm around my shoulder, "so hey, how was your day?" – *did I just get here?* Maybe he was right, the gym must help him become human again. Eagerly and hungrily, I suggest, "Is there something I can do to get dinner started?" He counters with a quick redirect, "How about we play some music?" – Sure....dinner music? Ughhh. So, after roughly ten minutes of listening to 80's light rock, I suggested we check on the chicken and its thawing progress. Frank popped up off the couch like he had forgotten about the idea of dinner, and I waited patiently. I could see him in the kitchen removing the three food items from the fridge to prepare, but I felt strange just sitting in the other room, so I moseyed into the kitchen.

He was stationed to the left of the sink, with a cutting board on the counter in front of him. I perched myself on the right side of the sink to give him space atop a somewhat clean counter surface. He first removed the chicken from its wrapping and placed it on the cutting board, grabbed a knife, and slowly cut into the mostly thawed breast, although you could still hear the iciness upon cutting. Each time he made a slice, chicken juice would ooze out onto the cutting board. I tried to initiate small talk, ask about work… family… just trying to get to know him more because we'd only met a few weeks ago, and I felt awkward sitting in another room during the dinner prep. But then something horrid happened – once he finished cutting the chicken into slices, he threw it into a large Tupperware container, immediately grabbed the kitchen (sink) towel, and proceeded to *wipe* the cutting board with this towel… spreading the chicken juice astray, all over the counter. He replaced the towel back to the edge of the sink. Then, without a thought of soap, sponge, or even water – he reaches for the next food item – the pepper! I had to be vigilant about disguising my wide eyes because I felt he was not the type that was open to constructive criticism about food safety and overall cleanliness, to say the least. I covered my mouth and kept my eyes low as he sliced the pepper and added it to the container. Again, grasping the sink towel to *tidy-up* the now mixed Salmonella- pinkish appearing juice running off the cutting board and down the front drawer. Painstakingly, he moved on to the onion, where I thought the nightmare would end. Once all items were cut, he moved the Tupperware out of the area and placed the cutting board in the sink…(this is good, this is good so far, I'm thinking)…But then, he grabs the towel for the final time…the sopping discolored towel, and wipes the counter in front of him in its entirety – absorbing/spreading the now Salmonella-pinkish-oniony juice across the counter. I remember he was talking about *something* at this point, but I have zero idea what it was – I couldn't focus, I was cringing inside – and yet somehow, I was more worried that he would notice my disgust, which would make him uncomfortable. Then, for no identifiable reason, Frank made way over to *my* side of the sink, towel in hand – I hopped off the counter like it was a hot potato and stared in angst as he proceeded to take the *filthy towel* and now spread its grotesque contents onto the right side (safe side) of the sink! This towel sure did get a workout, and so did my patience – I was exhausted! Without avail, he grabbed the Tupperware of food, turned to me, and said, "How do you want it cooked?" – Instantly, I said, "Well- done, char it!" – I exhaled when he slipped out the back patio door to light the grill, and wished there was somewhere to hide. God only knows what that grill looked like under the cover, but I had zero ambition to investigate. No, Frank was not a member of the FBI – rather, his name stands for "Foodborne Illness Frank," and he earned it.

I excused myself to use the bathroom and found more to treasure. Unfortunately, one of my discoveries was two ants on the toilet seat – and yes, that can happen, but what are the odds it's all happening to me tonight? I was scared to look around, but couldn't help but notice the black and white wallpaper, with flecks of gold glitter throughout – the Italian, it has to be! A second door within the bathroom led to his bedroom, which I noticed had *fire engine* red carpet and a dimly lit light. *Are you thinking what I'm thinking?* Yep. I had to…I just *had* to investigate. I took two steps into the bedroom and immediately peered up to notice a zebra-patterned wallpaper border around the room. When I told my brother this story, he rolled his eyes and said, "Oh geez, maybe the house came with the border, and he didn't change it yet" – but oh no, that was not the case because it matched the zebra decorative pillows on the bed! I was bewildered, peering around this room – I mean, what's happening in here?! There were two bureaus in the room, but the *fronts* of every drawer and cabinet were removed and stacked against the wall. So, you could literally *see* the folded clothes in these drawers and cabinets layered but not covered. But why? And yet again, black lacquer furniture, covered in dust – with additional dried flowers sporadically placed around the room. There were so many pondering questions in my brain, ones I knew I could never ask.

I convinced myself not to think of the condition of the grill where the chicken was being cooked – *just kiss it up to God and eat it,* I thought. Upon Frank's return with dinner, somewhere around 9:30pm, give or take, he directed me into the living room to eat. The kitchen table, if you can picture this, was covered with containers of powdered protein, shakers, Quaker Oats, peanut butter and fruit – all atop towels, placed to protect the surface, maybe? Either way, there was no shot of him moving these items, even though, again, he invited me to his house for a meal. Can you guess where we sat? On the filthy carpet in the living room, eating on top of the dusty, glass coffee table covered with his mail. I fought through dinner, chugged my beer, and hoped for the best. The rest of the night was eventless and short-lived, I had seen enough for sure. The more we talked, the more his ego came to light – which I couldn't listen to any longer, especially while being surrounded by filth. Giving myself undeserved credit, I did tell him over the phone that I wasn't interested in pursuing anything further. His response seemed surprised, maybe he hadn't been let down too often. I tried to shy away from detailed explanations, which felt critical and mean. For me, the "game over" flags seemed simple enough…basic household upkeep issues, lifestyle schedule differences…but at 44 years of age, such changes in simple habits should not have to happen and most likely wouldn't happen. I saved myself quite a few headaches. I had to bid farewell to FBI Frank.

"NOT-SO-SLICK-RICK"

Source of the Merger: Online

Just when you think you know someone. Surprise!

This will be the least comical chapter of all – mainly because it was my last attempt at investing time and energy into a man. The thought of updating my online profile, *yet again*, was a nauseating feeling. *Why am I even doing this anymore?* Faithfully, I updated pictures to reflect my current age, weight (which most men shockingly needed to confirm) and, of course, my extreme, unwavering *vibrancy*... Even though the exhaustion level of this process had reached its peak! Updating was a great attempt to hide my disdain for the fake profiles encountered for over 15 years, with some men advertising the *same* profile picture throughout these years...pants on fire! Early on in my online dating years, I felt compelled to reply to *all messages*. Whether I was completely disinterested or not, if someone took the time to reach out and send a complimentary message, I felt ignoring the message would be rude. After roughly a year of *that* pressure, I gave up responding – I realized if I'm not even the least bit interested, don't throw the bone because then it turns into a back- and-forth of nonsense conversation that I would never typically begin. Just to be nice? Nope.

So, back to Rick, an early "bite" after I updated my profile. From the first glance at his profile, he was handsome, athletic, family-oriented, well-spoken (written), and had a slight wit of humor, which was much appreciated. His initial messages were very straightforward – asking for my number, when can we meet, blah blah blah. We spoke very early on and hit it off, personality-wise. My one-word description of Rick early on was *wholesome*. He was very family- oriented, he was passionate about his career, coach of the year, son of the year, respectful, considerate...the whole nine!

On the way to our first date, he called me, he was petrified that I was going to *stand him up*. He asked to stay on the phone with me until I parked, and he could see that I was real – now, yesssss this seemed extremely bizarre to me, but it was almost adorable to see his vulnerability and how I might be that important to someone before we even met. This made me even more nervous...is *he* real?? *Why is he so worried?* As I stepped out of my car, I looked ahead of me to see one of the most attractive men I've ever seen walking towards me. Let me just take a minute to explain the word *attractive*. Even the most unfortunate-looking people can be attractive. Attractiveness encompasses your posture and how you carry yourself, the way you stand at rest, how your clothes fit you and how you wear them, a kind expression, a mix of shy and sexy – your level of attractiveness is not based at all on height, weight, or any other physical features, it's merely your presence. Does this breakdown make me sound *picky or shallow?* I imagine many readers would indeed have that thought – but just think about it for a moment. I don't know quite when it began or how what I believe to be a skill developed. I am just thankful for my visual perception ability because it has infamously saved me from even more short stories of anguish!

As we walked toward each other, he literally fell on me to hug me. I felt so lucky to feel that some way. We went into the restaurant and were seated. He put his menu down and asked if it would be alright if he "just looked at me for a minute." I wanted to crawl under the table...this absolute smoke show wanted to *just look at me?* Our first date was amazing, followed by multiple others. For the next month, I drove home from each date completely smitten.

Rick brought up the future often, "We're not getting any younger, and you're what I want." – I introduced him to my family after a few months of dating, and he reciprocated shortly after. My family really enjoyed him, but more importantly, they were relieved to see me *happy*. His parents were very sweet and made me feel so welcomed. I could tell he was their prince and very much the rock of his family, which was another admirable trait. He had apparently been "mistreated" in previous relationships; reports of being spoken to with *foul language,* affection not reciprocated, little things which caused a break-up...these stories made me sometimes wonder because he was always the victim. Mini flag? He was very close to his Mom, which I thought was an endearing quality. When I met her, she seemed fabulous. But something that puzzled me was that he stayed at his parents' house almost full-time. He owned his own home, which was even closer to his job than his parent's home – but he was never there. I mean, he was never ever there. If we stopped over there, he would have mail piled to the sky! On more than one occasion, I asked, "Why don't you live in your own house?" – "I don't like it here," he would respond. I never poked further because I felt like maybe it was a reminder of an ex, but as the months went on, there was never a clear answer to this question.

Our first *sleepover* raised a small red flag. We traveled an hour or two away to have dinner, a nice room at a hotel, and a hike in the morning, blah blah blah. He brought a bottle of champagne, which was sweet, considerate, and felt romantic. *I was really looking forward to a little getaway.* I'm sure some would agree with my excitement...being away from home, knowing no one else, being alone with the one you care about...fill in the blanks here. To my surprise, though, after coming back from dinner and popping the champagne, Rick wanted to watch TV in bed surrounded by pillows (which did not include me) and go to sleep. I remembered rolling over, feeling like I had been gut-punched, blaming myself. *What is my outfit? Is he tired?* He's always saying he's tired. *Is it me?* I thought back to how he had broken up with someone because they neglected to give him adequate affection – what is adequate? How about *any* affection? Can I get some? Haha. Somehow, I fell asleep despite not being able to shake the feeling that he didn't find me attractive. Again, being incapable of hiding my confusion, I gently mentioned the missed opportunity of "alone time" the next morning. Rick dismissed my feelings, repeatedly saying how tired he was and that I "should drop it." Consider it dropped, *along with my confidence.*

When I first met his parents, I think he was relieved that I got the *thumbs up*. He seemed so excited, "Hey listen, this will happen quick...it's gonna be a ring, a house, and babies!" Most women would have lit up, literally. As I had mentioned before, women are usually pegged for initiating *future* talks... weddings, babies, all of it. But not in this scenario. He brought it up constantly, I never once initiated a conversation about a plan for the future. He was actively looking for land to build our own house...scoping my area to relocate his job...and told his parents to prepare for a wedding. Our time was so limited due to our schedules that weekends were the only time we had together.

We proceeded to spend the next two holidays together, Thanksgiving and Christmas – where he met my extended family...not an easy feat, as I had been solo for over 5 years before this. Everyone loved him, family and friends...what was there not to like? The New Year was another holiday together, and again, so many plans were discussed for our next year together. Our first Valentine's Day was anticlimactic, mostly because he wanted to stay in – so I made dinner, and we had a nice night. Again, with the nonexistent affection – barely anything – and what's with all the pillows everywhere building a wall to keep me out? *Was he tired again? Was it the salmon? Did he not like women?* – my brain! Little did I know that the next morning would be the last time I saw Not-So-Slick-Rick.

Because our time was limited to weekends, I always made plans to ensure we could make the most of our time together. But just once, after 7 months, I had asked him to make the plans –

Me: "What do you wanna do this weekend? Should I come there? Did you want to come here?"

Rick: "I don't care."

Me: "What are you in the mood to do?"

Rick: (annoyed) "I don't know, I really don't care, just tell me what we're doing."

Hey guys/gals – if this task is too much for you, then you are just not interested in seeing the person, right? Right. Little did I know that our first (and last) disagreement would ensue. Clearly, I was not asking for a lot here, in fact, I could be one of the lowest- maintenance partners ever. In hindsight, I realized I had planned every date, movie, activity, holiday event, and sleepover we enjoyed. I cooked any meal he wanted, answered nightly phone calls for him to vent about *his* day, supported his busy schedule, bought the most considerate and thoughtful gifts for his birthday and holidays, and never monopolized his free time with expectations of plans for us. All I asked was for Rick to plan an activity for the *less than 24 hours* we were about to spend together. There was grumbling on the other end of the phone, and he hung up.

Seven days later, after countless unanswered texts and phone calls – I finally broke down and sent a text to his Mother...oh yes, yes, I did. I was worried, what if something happened to him? We were both driving during our last conversation – maybe something awful happened? *Hi Mrs. (blah blah) – I haven't heard from Rick in a week, he hasn't returned any of my texts or phone calls...is he ok?.* She did not respond, but within an hour, my phone rang. There he is – sounding solemn, annoyed, and dismissive. When previously I was looking for a pulse, now I am enraged that he has one! Not only does he have a pulse, its also piggy-backed with a pretentious attitude.

Me: "What's going on? Why have you been ignoring me?"

Rick: "So what? We got in a fight; I didn't feel like talking."

Me: "Our first argument, and you ghost me? How old are you? Are you serious?"

Rick: "I didn't feel like talking. I didn't break up with you. Whatever."

Me: "Ohh, you think we're still together? That's a riot."

The *person* on the other end of that phone wasn't the person that I knew. In fact, I had never heard that tone of voice before, coupled with his one-word immature responses. Who was this person? It felt like a 15-year-old boy and his Mom having a disagreement. *Whatever. Uh-huh, yeah, sure. Yea ok. Whatever.* My mind was blown. And is this deserved behavior after such a minor disagreement? What will happen if we ever have a *real* problem or a *real* disagreement. There was nothing *slick* about Rick, that's for sure – and I made sure every peculiar red flag was mentioned during our last conversation.

After all, what else did I have to lose? Not a thing. From the outside, he was a perfect specimen who could make a heart melt, but what was inside did not match...it leaked out and rose to the surface. The truth always will.

"HIS NAME WAS RANDY"

Source of the Merger: Online

Attempting to lighten the mood after the previous hardship above, I bring you Randy. Randy was, thankfully, my very last online interaction. Shortly after Randy and I began to message online, we exchanged numbers. He wanted to meet up quickly to get a litmus test on this thing called chemistry, and I was in! At this point, I had zero expectations, and I mean zero. A goal, though, is to get the *meet and greet* done in case there is no shot at moving forward. But just as suspected and proven to me on repeat, I could tell there was a sense of entitlement by the 5th text or so. I can hear all of you... "Oh, stop, just give the guy a chance, you didn't even meet yet!" And you're right, but after 20 years of this nonsense, it's considered *substantial experience.*

He says, "I like to keep it light, so let's start with a walk somewhere." Ok, I understand... the transition of strategical dates has been quite an evolution - years ago, it was dinner, then it became "drinks and apps," then it morphed into "just a drink," shortly after it became "coffee"...and now, just a walk in the park. It behooves me to discuss the obvious, which would be the financial burden of a more expensive date, which most men feel they have to be the ones to take on. But something critical to note is the length of time allotted for these first dates – and trust me, I absolutely recognize instances when *the shorter, the better* just fits..., but in changing the vibe of the date, you're also changing or limiting the level of interaction.

I agreed to a *walk,* but when inclement weather would be greeting us at the said walk, he suggested meeting at a mall to walk around. That was a hard "no" for me. *Walk around in a mall and talk? As strangers?* No. And Lord help me, I can't even picture this. Would we be walking side-by-side (of course), so we would be staring at each other and trying to nonchalantly interrogate one another? We would have to be mindful of the senior citizens who were enjoying this same activity in a safe environment with appropriate AC. I'll pass on this one. Then, Randy suggested a Saturday, but I only had a brief early afternoon window to offer. He agrees, and the weather should be fine, so we're rerouting back to the park. The night before, he texted and asked me if I would be interested in going bowling instead. *The bowling again.* But hey, I feel a little better that he's choosing to do an activity, so I agree. He was going to pick a bowling alley between us, and we would meet. Thennnn, in the morning, roughly 4 hours before our date, he asks if it would be alright if we hit an alley closer to him – "My brakes are bad, and I'm getting them fixed Monday". Got it. Just strange, though, right? Of course, I graciously agree – and head to the alley of choice.

The first curiosity for me was the location – online, his "residence" was not near this bowling alley. In fact, the location we were heading to was in a blighted area. Nope, I wasn't scared, just perplexed. I pull into the parking lot about 15 minutes before the date, with only 4 other cars in attendance. Two men were having a wheelchair race out front in the parking lot...a race! – *where am I?* Stealthily, I take a quick glance around the lot and peer into each car – only 2 of them are difficult to see into, but from what I can see, I'm the only soul in a vehicle. I texted Randy and let him know I was there, just chillin' in the parking lot. Eight minutes pass...no one is going in or coming out of the alley – and I'm keeping my head on a swivel in the lot for sure! Finally, an unsaved number texts me...

Randy: "Hey, it's Randy, this is my other phone."

Me: "You have another phone?"

Randy: "Yeah, my other one isn't working. I'm here, walking to the door."

Me: "......"

I looked up at the door...nothing. Back at all the cars...nothing. Am I at the right place??

Then, the driver's door opens from a car out yonder – one that could not be viewed into. Out steps Randy...in a worn, navy blue Chevrolet t-shirt and black running shorts with a white stripe, freckled with stains. Immediately, I could feel the disappointment, and apparently, I didn't hide it so well. I wasted yet another cute outfit for this one.

Randy: "Did you ever see that commercial when they're on a date, and the stain is talking so the girl can't even concentrate on what he's saying?"

Me: "Yep. Did you see the one when a couple is on a date, and she comments, 'You look very comfortable' – because his shirt looks like he rolled out of a hamper?"

We both chuckled but quickly started moving toward the door. After apologizing for his attire, he admitted that he almost *overslept* our date – it was 2pm...who is *still* sleeping at 2pm? When we entered the doors, you could hear a pin drop – there may have been 6 people in the whole place, including the staff. We mosey over to the counter to get our lane set up…and here comes the dreaded moment (or one of them). *Who reserves the lane? His card? My card? What are the demands?* The panic. Alas, as soon as we stepped to the counter, Randy handed the cashier his card. Crisis averted, so I think.

We get our shoes and get set in a lane closest to the wall. It's thankfully dark to hide the stains and shame. As I slip my first foot into those fabulous slick shoes, Randy belts out, "Isn't healthcare a joke? I mean, the whole profession, the concept – we have control of our own bodies, people just need to take care of them." *What are we embarking on? Did someone recently suggest you need medication or something? How was this triggered?* But calmly, I continued to slip into the death shoes and proceed with this first (and final) date! Within seconds, he pops up ready to roll – but says, "I'm thirsty, do you think they have a water fountain here?" – *A What?? A water fountain? Are we in elementary school? What adult drinks from a water fountain?* Better yet, what adult seeks out a water fountain when directly behind him is a concession stand filled with staggeringly cold refreshments? Even if you didn't want to *buy* a bottle of water, just ask for a cup… of safe…water. Nope. He briskly walked the entirety of the bowling alley just to get a few seconds, or gulps, of a mediocre room-temperature water fountain. I watched him walk the entire way. I have zero recollection of what my face was doing, but it couldn't have been good. Good Lord. How many more times did he take this trip, you ask? Four. Four more times, he walked the length of the bowling alley to quench his thirst. *Was I thirsty?* Maybe. *Did he ask if I was hungry or thirsty?* No. *Did I mind?* No, because during his next few walks to the fountain, I utilized the time to remain sane, take some deep breaths, and stay positive.

The conversations were difficult, but I did try. Randy felt like his athletic ability superseded all professional athletes; "they were fools." However, he also felt licensure and/or certifications that included any type of "letters after your name" were also hogwash. He fully agreed that women should *not* make decisions regarding their own bodies but was eager to touch mine. Randy openly asked if he could touch my leg…*touch my leg?* If there are any men reading that can picture themselves in this situation, *can you imagine asking this question?* Firstly, if you must ask, then you clearly have no shot in coming near my leg. Secondly, his comment included, "You look like you're muscular, but can I touch your leg and see?" Do not do this. Please do not do this to anyone. **Dating Tip #7:** If you are unsure of a person's physicality when you're literally in person, don't reveal this. Glare at them when they walk to the bathroom…check them out when they are glancing up at a waiter when ordering. Figure it out, but do not ask if you can touch them, it is hands-down bizarre. To piggy-back, when the initial comment about a physical feature doesn't "hit" the way you would like, please do not follow up the way Randy did. Randy's next comment was about my hips. Now, fellas and ladies – if you want to throw a hip compliment out to a woman, there are multiple *mindful* ways to land it with success without stripping them of dignity. Randy, however, led with, "You have the kind of hips every man would like to put a seed in." Pump. The. Brakes. *Can you fathom this comment?* Please think about this for a moment. You, sir, at the age of 45, have not been successful in planting a seed anywhere, in anyone – and yet your tiny brain felt speaking this thought aloud would compliment me? Did you assume you would utilize my hips for seed implantation? Randy, stop.

With all my power and might, I tried to power through this date, inevitably knowing this would be the first and last outing. After multiple inappropriate suggestions and comments, the date was finally over. We headed toward the payment center, Godspeed, which I thought had been covered by the inviting party. My conscience could not allow Ryan's full payment – as I handed my card to the cashier to *go Dutch*. Randy whips out five $20 bills and fans them while in line as if we were in a casino.

Me: "What are you doing? Don't they have your card?"

Randy: "Yeah, but I have all this cash."

I asked the cashier to split our bill, which Randy did not refute. Shockingly, the 17-year-old cashier was apparently confused, put the entire tab on my card, and handed me the receipt to sign. I begrudgingly look up and say, "Is this the whole bill?" She says yes, and swiftly, Randy grabs his card and places it in his wallet. In addition, he folds up his once-fanned $20 bill collection, places it into his pocket and says, "I guess I'll pay for the next date." *Like hell, you will, Randy. Hasta nunca.*

Although I left that building with yet another great story, it felt like I endured a marathon of inappropriate comments and overall utter malarkey. His misappropriated confidence and entitlement were astounding, blinding, if you will. Ryan was the literal straw that broke the camel's back.

Never since have I dabbled into the online variety. I waved the white flag, not in defeat, but without the intention to pursue it. To quote Hemmingway, "A man can be destroyed but not defeated." The *guess who* was on the other side of the dating app was over. That day, I returned home and blissfully deleted all my online dating accounts.

FUN EXTRAS

FLAKEY FRANK – Another wonderful Frank to speak of, whom I met online. Frank: Handsome, charismatic, handy, owned a home, no crazy exes (that I was aware of), no children (that I was aware of). I should have seen a warning flag when, on our first date, he asked if he could touch my waist to inspect if I had *rolls*. Rolls? "Well, your sweater is baggy. Girls hide their bodies on first dates, and I just wanted to make sure." Again, with this, *can I touch you* stuff. *Awkwardly*, I laughed and grabbed my own waist to show him...ironically it was *I* who felt embarrassed, but not the man who looked like he needed a steak and an Ensure® – I mean, I could've snapped him like a twig – and he's worried about me hiding rolls? It's unreal thinking back on it now. For our second date, I met a few of his closest friends, had a great time, and he seemed happy to have me at the event. On the third date, he introduced me to his sister...we had another great time, and everything seemed alright. So, the fourth date was going to just be him and I – he invited me to his home (I know, I know...don't panic). His home was diametrically opposite to that of FBI Frank – super clean, organized, furnished! To jump right to it and keep this brief, I brought over fixings to make margaritas. We sat down to watch a movie, he had a few sips...and promptly, he FELL ASLEEP. Like sound asleep, I was barely able to wake him up to inform him I was leaving. I texted him the next day to see if he was ok – and he ghosted me – a complete flake, a Flakey Frank. **Dating Tip #8:** Do not introduce someone new to your close friends or family within the first 3 weeks, or at least until you can assess your likelihood of ghosting them. All in all, it just leaves a sour taste and unwanted pressure on the person – for no reason. It also doesn't shed the best light on yourself, either.

TINY TIM – Tim was a very handsome online match who I spoke to for roughly a week before we met in person. I was excited about this date... a good personality job, and seemed family-oriented – seriously, the "top 5's" begin to change as the years go by – *having a job* is the new prerequisite these days! I pull up at the restaurant, rocking a super cute and casual dress, flat boots and high aspirations. Tim parked a few cars down, but when I got out of my car to walk towards him, I couldn't see him – *wait, wasn't he just in the car? Where did he go?* – Oh, there he is...his hair just breaking the plane of the car next to me. Wait a minute, wait a minute...*his profile said 5'10, right? Did I see that right? Was I dreaming?* All of a sudden, there he is, with a shy yet confident smile. Here I go...*try to act like he didn't lie to me, just try.* See, here's the thing, if there are little mysteries about you, and you'd like to remain ambiguous about certain details of your life before you get to know someone, I *totally* understand – I mean, they have to make the cut, right? Right. But I have a *real* problem with men that lie about their height. It is unequivocally the *first* thing women notice, the very first thing. Who wants to start the date off with a lie? I intentionally wear flat heels on first dates for this exact reason, isn't that sad? I wear flats to corroborate their stated height. And I LOVE it when they tell the truth. I don't care if you're 5'5 or 6'2...just don't lie about it. It helps no one, and you lose points before you can even open a door for me. He mentioned his union job, and based on his age, I happened to know someone in the same union, the same age. But Tim was not familiar – he said, "How old is he?" I say, "he's our age, he's 32", my age at the time. Blankly, he looked at me, "Ohhh, I'm not 32, I'm 42 – it's so weird it wouldn't let me change my birthdate online". What. I drop my eyes, but only briefly. *That's lie #2.* "Why would you have to *change* your birthdate, though? Did you enter it incorrectly the first time??" I snarled. **Dating Tip #9:** Lying about your height and age could be the most absentminded strategy – that no woman will ever fall for. How do you incorrectly enter your birth year on a website? Call me crazy, but it's more of a reflex when I'm entering my birthdate – how can you mess that up? I honestly cannot recall the rest of the date, as I had checked out within the first 30 minutes and could not refresh. I split the check and dipped it as fast as possible.

DIVORCED DAN

– This will be the briefest tale to tell. Dan and I met online, and he immediately wanted to meet for a drink...like within 24hrs. Typically, I prefer more time, as you can see from previous stories – but I threw my hands up and said, ehhh. Dan told me prior to our visit that he was divorced with 2 children and did not want to waste time *getting to know* someone if the physical connection was off. He invited me to meet him for a drink at 6pm, which is, to me, a normal time to begin a date, or so I thought. I pull up a casual but cute outfit in effect...Dan steps out of his truck covered in dirt, ripped jeans (not purposefully) and boots covered in dry mud...clearly, he came right from work. Even though I do enjoy the blue-collar rugged type, maybe he wasn't so worried about that physical attraction previously mentioned? To keep this account short and simple – within 30 minutes of this date, Dan's story went from an employed, bill-payin', house-ownin,' divorced, single father of 2 - to an employed, (possibly) bill-payin', divorced, father of 3 (the youngest being 6 months old), living in his mamma's basement. Check, please. **Dating Tip #10:** If you are a proud parent, there is *never* a need to conceal the truth about the number of children you have. He is *not* the first man to do this. I'm sure he wasn't exactly proud of his situation at the time, but with the youngest child being 6 months old, trying to begin a new relationship may not be the smartest next adventure. Just sayin'.

www.ingramcontent.com/pod-product-compliance
Lightning Source LLC
Chambersburg PA
CBHW050728010526
44107CB00009B/781